Be Patient
Be Present
Be Joyful

A First-Aid Kit *for the* Emotional
Bumps, Scrapes, *and* Bruises of Life

Ryan M. Stanley

© 2018 Ryan Stanley. All rights reserved.

No part of this book may be used or reproduced in any manner whatsoever without the express written permission of the publisher or author. The exception would be in the case of brief quotations embodied in critical articles or reviews, and pages where permission is specifically granted by the publisher or author, or in the case of photocopying, a licence from Access Copyright, www.accesscopyright.ca, 1-800-893-5777, info@accesscopyright.ca.

Library of Canada Cataloguing in Publication data is available.

ISBN: 978-0-9936367-9-0 (Hardcover Edition)
ISBN: 978-1-989528-00-6 (Paperback Edition)
ISBN: 978-1-989528-01-3 (E-book Edition)

First Edition Printing 2019

Editing by Lorraine Gane
Front cover image, illustrations, and hand-lettering
by Laura Lavender
Book design by Clint Hutzulak, Rayola Creative

PRINTED AND BOUND IN CANADA
Published in Canada by Above the Noise, Victoria, BC
www.abovethenoisepublishing.com
For more information contact: publishing@abovethenoise.ca

Special discounts are available on quantity purchases by corporations, associations, and others. For details, contact the publisher at the address above.

For more information on the book and author please visit
www.RyanStanley.com

"To change
the world,"
replied the muse.

...And it was true.

Prologue: You are a creator

Occasionally while traveling on the sunny road of this adventure we call life, a dark cloud will pass over and block the sun.

Two things to remember:
1. its temporary
2. those dark clouds contain rain which is essential not only for growth but for life itself.

Hey, are you okay? Sit down. Take a breather. Let's get you taken care of.

Ready? Alright. Here we go.

First things first. Before we even begin this first aid process, it's important for you to know that You are a creator. Yes, you. You are creating in every moment of every day and have been since the moment you were conceived. If you are going to get the most benefit, and in the author's opinion the most effective use and value from reading this flock of words, cleverly disguised as a marketable, readable first-aid kit, you will need to either have complete buy-in on this concept of *you being a creator*, or at the very least suspend any disbelief. Kind of like before you open a physical, medical first-aid kit you already know for a fact that although bandages, Neosporin, and duct tape can heal any minor wound it will be your body that takes care of the healing.

Seriously though, YOU are a creator.

Whatever you're doing right now, you are creating. When you speak, you are creating words and conversation. When you put bacon, lettuce, and tomato on some slightly toasted bread with a little slab of mayo and a little salt and pepper, you just created a delicious BLT. We create conversations, art of all types, friendships, music, laughter, fear, businesses, adventures, and life. That's right. We are always and in all ways creating our own LIFE. By wearing a certain outfit, you may be creating a man

Your dreams and ideas
are the seeds of the
✦✦ ✦ universe. ✦ ✦ ✦
water them. give them light.
Most importantly,
GIVE THEM TIME TO GROW.

Eventually, they will become—
⎯something bigger, stronger
— and more beautiful —
than you could ever imagine.

or a woman dressed in blue. By reading this, you are literally creating a person reading a book. So just by being, we are creating. By being angry, we are creating an angry person. By being happy, we are creating a happy person. By being thankful, we are creating gratitude. When we begin to choose what and who we create in our everyday experiences from a detached perspective, and we are aware we always have that choice, we begin to build the mental and conscious muscle that gives us control over our thoughts, consistently and with purpose. The more we control our thoughts, the more we understand how we are actually creating our experience and the perception of that experience based on those thoughts. Crazy stuff right?

In the meantime, life happens. More often than not, our thoughts are having a free for all, running around in our noggin and dragging whatever emotions they see fit along the way. Life is certainly an adventure and can often be an emotional one at that. *Occasionally,* we somehow create stressed, anxious or worried people. For the sake of congruence with the title of this first-aid kit, let's call these feelings of stress, anxiety, and worry our "emotional bumps, scrapes, and bruises" of life.

What many people don't realize is when we're out participating in this crazy adventure called life on a daily basis and these emotional bumps, scrapes, and bruises occur, there are always opportunities for us to go to our own internal first-aid kit of patience,

When you give unconditionally,
life provides you with more
opportunities to give.
To do that it must, in turn,
give you more opportunities to recieve,
so you have more to give.
It's an invisible cycle of awesomeness
that nature invites you to participate in daily.

presence, and joy to heal these injuries and intentionally create a calmer, more intentional person and way of being.

Obviously, **self-mastery is a life-long journey**, but my intention is that the following suggestions in the form of very small chapters will serve as first aid for any sudden or lasting emotional bumps, scrapes, and bruises you may be experiencing right now.

Are you ready? Good. Thank You.

Take three deep slow breaths.

When you do this, oxygen fills your lungs, which distribute it to your blood cells and brings extra oxygen to your body and brain. You probably knew that already, I just wanted to emphasize I was being serious about the deep breaths thing and that it is part of the first-aid process.

Okay. One more time. *Breathe* deep.

Smile.

Breathe deep *again*.

Think of someone or something you are especially grateful for.

Let's begin.

Chapter 1: Be Patient

— Patience —
attracts happiness
it brings near that
which is far.
swahili proverb

Patience can be your best friend if you let it. One of the biggest challenges in today's first-world society is the need for immediacy and with that the constant common dissatisfaction for any form of waiting.

If you're feeling stress about something, there's a good chance that time, or your perspective there is not enough of it, is somehow involved. Even if that is just wanting to feel better about something else *right now*.

What can you control as a creator? Can you control time? Theoretically, but that's not where I'm going with this.

What you can control is how you respond to a fear of there not being enough time.

Be patient. Take a moment to breathe. Stress comes from being attached to an outcome. Take a moment to realize the outcome will occur as it's supposed to, when it's supposed to. That doesn't mean sit back and do nothing. On the contrary. Take action towards your desired outcome as a patient person, with no hurry to have it all happen right now, and you'll actually be able to see the pieces of the puzzle falling into place more clearly because you won't be so busy energetically staring at the clock of life.

The only thing between you and your desired outcome is time. *Who* you choose to create during that time is literally up to *you* in each moment.

Choose to create who you want to be in this moment and create a you that is patient.

Life is for living.
The road may
wind or narrow.
Keep going.
There are wide open
spaces on the other side
— of persistance. —

Be patient. When you are no longer in a hurry, you no longer feel pressure of the unknown. You are in charge of the moment and you are in control of who you are in that moment. Decide you can choose to spend this time between now and then **any way you want**.

Create a patient person. Create a person who is being patient.

Ask yourself:

- *What does patience feel like?*
- *What does a patient person feel like?*
- *How would I behave if I were creating a patient person right now?*

You want something to be different than it is right now. I understand that. What can you control about that? You can control your thoughts and decide to stop and think about patience and how it serves you and your desired outcome right now more than impatience does. Interestingly enough, just by choosing to pause and be curious about what patience feels like, you are in a sense already creating some patience and therefore a patient person. Nice job!

Breathe in again. Then close your eyes for a moment and think about the patient person you are about to create.

Band Aids

- *Patience is a choice*
- *Shift your mindset from focusing on a lack of time to one that creates a patient person*
- *Who you choose to create is up to you in each moment*
- *The outcome will occur exactly as it's supposed and when it's supposed to.*
- *You are the author of your story.*
- *You are in charge of your life.*

Chapter 2: Be Present

If the sight of the
blue skies fills you with joy
if a blade of grass springing up in the fields
has power to move you,
if the simple things of nature
have a message that you
— understand —
rejoice, for your soul is alive

Eleonora Duse

Be Present. Stress and anxiety often come from attachment to a specific outcome in the future or what you or someone else did/didn't do, said/didn't say, at some point in the past, or even what someone else, somewhere else believes about you or someone who is important to you. Take a moment to ask yourself, "Am I worried or stressed about something that happened in the past or, perhaps I believe will happen in the future?" "Am I concerned about what someone else, somewhere else believes?" Ninety-nine percent of the time the answer will be yes. So what can you do about that?

Be Present.

Now that you have created patience, and an understanding of what a patient person feels like, you are not waiting on anything or fearful of not having enough time. Take a moment to ***be present.***

Literally take a moment, right now, to look at everything surrounding you for the actual epic awesomeness that it is. Go ahead. Look around you. What do you see right here, right now?

You can create someone who literally sees beauty in every single thing around him or her because in actuality it is all abundance sustaining your existence and your experience.

Breathing in
I calm body & mind
Breathing out, I smile.
Dwelling in the present moment
I know this is the only moment.

Thich Nhat Hanh

Look around. Be present.
Life is constantly
giving to you.
There are so many
stories going on in
our heads that
are not only untrue
but often serve to
distract us from
seeing the beauty of
every moment of our
existence.
Life is everywhere,
inviting you to make it
whatever you want it to
be.

Now think about the following questions:

- What does a present person think about?
- What does a completely present person see, smell, hear, taste, and physically feel?
- Have you ever taken a moment to intentionally feel the air against the skin of your face? Can you feel where your fingertips are holding this book?

Breathe in deep again.

Now close your eyes for a moment and think about the present person you are about to create.

When you open your eyes, look again at everything all around you and think about the magic that is actually and literally surrounding you at all times.

*Realize deeply
that the present moment
is all you have
— Make the NOW —
the primary focus of your life*

Eckhart Tolle

Choose your thoughts wisely.

You can literally think about anything you want.

Start with gratitude. What are you grateful for right now?

Here are a couple of suggestions for starters:

- Oxygen, sunlight, clothing, any human who makes you happy, running water, your pet, the fact you can read this.
- Consciousness! Awareness!
- Hugs. High Fives.
- Trees, birds, the beauty of emotional pain. Life is an EXPERIENCE!

Every moment is literally a miracle. Be Here. Be Present. Be Grateful. This is the only now you have.

Be patient.

Be present.

If you do this as often as possible the rest falls into place. I'm not saying it's always easy, I am saying it's always possible. It's all about awareness and choice. Like any other muscle in the body, building this muscle of presence and awareness of the Now will enhance your ability to utilize it as often as you like, with efficiency and effectiveness and eventually with what feels like no effort at all.

Breathe in deep again.

Life begins where your comfort zone ends.
You've got ONE LIFE
What are you doing with it?
Do things that scare you until they don't scare you anymore
That is where greatness lives.

Oxygen,

sunlight,

gravity,

water (in solid, liquid or gas forms),

plants,

animals,

insects,

the earth itself,

clouds,

the wind.

It's all here right now…for you, so you can live and be here now.

I didn't mean to get so heavy so fast, but seriously, think about it!

It's all just matter being morphed by our thoughts and perception. Create someone who chooses their perception in the "now." Know that "now" is all there actually is and when we're not being present, we're often ruining "now" with a fear about the past or a future that may or may not even exist.

You are better than that. *Life* is better than that. Focus on the beauty of the now and what you can do in it.

Band Aids

- *Gratitude fuels presence*
- *Spend time with and in nature*
- *Take slow breathes and think about the oxygen filling your lungs*
- *Pay attention to what all five of your senses are experiencing right now*

chapter 3:
Be Joyful

If you carry joy in your heart you can heal any moment.

Carlos Santana

Be Joyful.

Now that you are patient and present, how else would you rather be feeling? I'm not suggesting that when you're upset, anxious or stressed it's always as easy as a flip of the switch to just "be positive" or "Don't worry, Be Happy" but believe it or not with practice, patience, and presence you can feel this way a lot of the time. At least enough for you to take control of the situation in the present moment.

You always have a choice: create a smile, stretch. Think about someone you love unconditionally. Joy is free. The more you intend for joy to be a part of your life, the more it starts to show up. Especially when you're able to be patient and present first.

The next time you are bored, decide to create a person who is authentically grateful for joy and see what happens.

If you are patient and present, then you are Here, Now.

What does the word joy mean to you?

Create a joyful moment.

Just one moment with more joy in it than the one preceding it.

*Every breath we take
every step we make
can be filled with
peace, joy & serenity*

— Thich Nhat Hahn —

Breathe deep. Look around. Create joy in your mind. If your creative engine needs some fuel, pour in a little more gratitude. Be grateful for anything: gravity, sunlight, oxygen, laughter… now smile and say "Thank You."

THERE! There it was! Did you feel that?!?! Of course, you did! You felt it because you created it!

Now do that again as often as you think of it, and gradually it will start to happen as if almost by itself. You may find yourself just wanting to be patient one day and joy will sneak in there and surprise you without any effort on your part. When that happens, say "Thank You" and you will automatically also become present!

Life literally surrounds us and provides everything we need to thrive. It changes with the seasons of experience, but it is still always and in all ways *everywhere*.

Be Patient.
Be Present.
Be Joyful.

Band Aids

- *Think about five people around whom you feel joyful*
- *Pet an animal*
- *Stretch/exercise/practice yoga*
- *Send someone a text telling them how much you appreciate them*
- *Create gratitude for anything or anyone*
- *Hug yourself*

Epilogue
Keep Going

Accept — then act.
Whatever the present moment contains,
Accept it as if you had chosen it.
Always work with it,
not against it.

— Eckhart Tolle —

Keep Going.

It's these two simple words that when put together in times of doubt will serve you in ways you may not even realize for years. They are, in a sense, a reminder that your purpose exists and you are still on that path if you say you are. In fact, the only way you can get off the path of your purpose is to not keep going.

Keep Going.

Life is malleable. A major ingredient in your ability to create any outcome in life is equal parts time and patience.

Keep Going.

By choosing to create with patience, presence, and joy, as often as possible, life becomes a constant opportunity for you to decide the pace at which you choose to move forward in the direction of the person you intend to be in every way. The more often your thoughts and actions point your experience in that direction, the less time and patience may be required for you to become that person. In any case, ***keep going***. On your toughest day, and on your easiest day. In your darkest hour, and in your most shining moment. Just say those two words and then follow through.

Every great dream begins with a dreamer. Always remember, you have within you the strength, the patience and the passion to reach for the stars to change the world.

— Harriet Tubmam —

Create a person who is still moving forward. It's okay you felt defeated. It's okay you had a stressful experience and reacted the way you did. Rest.

Be Patient. Be Present. Be Joyful....

Then Keep Going.

Every Moment in Life is a Gift.

This moment right now. Here. Now... is a gift. Keep going.

The gift of life is the most sacred thing there is. It is literally all there is. That can be a lot to handle. Your thoughts, the ones you were having right before you picked up this book and every thought since are some of the main ingredients of your experience in this sacred thing called Life. If your thoughts and actions are anxious, tired, angry, worried or scared, that's okay. If any other person had literally been born exactly when and where you were to your parents, and lived literally every single second of your life, having all of the same experiences you did, having all of the exact same thoughts about and reactions to those experiences as you did, they would be feeling the exact same way. That doesn't mean those anxious, tired, angry, worried or scared thoughts are serving your purpose though. It also doesn't mean that's who you have to be for the rest of your life, or even the rest of your day. Now you have an opportunity to choose to create a person

Life is a beautiful game
that can be fun, exhausting,
and challenging.
Feel the feelings
and play the game to the best of your ability.
Learn from your errors
and help others do the same.
Don't worry about what the score is,
for in the end people will only
remember how you played!

who is patient, present, joyful, and grateful for this moment of existence as there will never be another one like it.

Try it. Right now. I'll wait.

Take Three Deep Breaths.

I Am Patient.

I Am Present.

I Am Joyful.

Thank You.

Now…Keep Going.

If this first-aid kit has served you in any way, please consider paying that service forward by giving copies to friends who have had their share of bumps, scrapes, and bruises and could use a little first aid of their own.

CPR

The following are passages taken from various posts on the author's Instagram page, meant to be read as a quick fix or band aid for any minor bumps, scrapes, or bruises that may occur in your adventure of life. To see the photographs taken by the author that accompany each of these quick fixes, you can follow him on **Instagram @rms_ryanstanley.**

There are windy days in life that can blow the leaves off the branches of your soul. You can feel naked and alone. Be patient and know they will grow back, possibly bigger and more beautiful than before. Be present and grateful for the leaves that were there to begin with. Look around at all of the beauty of life that is absolutely still here, now, and which you might not have seen if those leaves were still there. Be joyful because you can. Joy is free and it's contagious.

※ ※ ※

There is more going on beyond the surface of your life than you could ever imagine. When you spend your time thinking about what you want to manifest in your life, millions if not billions of moving parts you will never ever see begin moving things and people into your path to bring about what you desire. And more often than not, in a way you would have never ever thought of.

※ ※ ※

I've found the more we acknowledge the language of life in the Universe that speaks to us every day, the more we see it and in turn, the more it wants to show up for us. What do you think?

When you choose to consistently seek light in life, even on the darkest of days, it will eventually shine on you so bright you'll know without question it is always shining for you. Everything happens for you. Look for the lesson. Once you love the lesson and the light, then shine your own light for all of the others on your path who believe they're alone in the dark.

I'm grateful for so much today (and every day) but on this Thanksgiving what I'm most grateful for is the power to choose which thoughts I give attention to. When you remember **you** are the author of your story and every thought you have is a part of that story, you take control of your life and you can make a difference in the life of every person you come in contact with. Choose your thoughts wisely. Choose how you spend the precious time you have in thought and in action. Bless yourself so you can bless others.

Ryan Stanley

The end of each and every day offers an opportunity for gratitude reflection, and growth: "What were my wins? What were my lessons? Who have I taught? Who have I learned from? How can I serve my purpose in a more intentional way tomorrow?"

✦ ✦ ✦

Life is so much bigger than we can ever imagine. We are the conductor and concertmaster of so many silent instruments that play the song of our existence. We get to choose the tempo and energy, but most of us sit and wait for someone else to lead the orchestra. For the sake of your life and the lives of those important to you, take the baton! Direct your life to the crescendo you want to experience!

✦ ✦ ✦

How often do you stop to truly celebrate life? How often do you take a moment to be present and look at the magic of your existence? Every single moment in life is not only a gift, but an opportunity to live in wonder at the fact that you actually exist and can feel the feelings and emotions of life! You are a miracle. Act like it!

Life is an adventure! Get out. Explore. It doesn't have to be by plane. Plan a day trip. Create opportunities for magic and miracles by taking yourself out of your routine. Once a week, once a month or once a year. Meet new people. See what/who life will put in your path when you shift the direction of your path.

✧ ✧ ✧

You are a unique piece of art. There is no one else exactly like you on this entire planet of billions. You've been given this life to live and to love. To give and to receive. What are you doing with this unique experience of consciousness? What will your legacy be?

✧ ✧ ✧

Everything you do and think about today creates your future. Every thought and conversation you have, every action you take has a powerful impact on the life you are creating. How much time do you spend thinking about the future you want to live in? There is a you in the future. You are in charge of what you will look and feel like. Decide every day who you want to be and be it with passion and determination.

Winds of life will come in, especially when you choose to live on the shores of your comfort zone. Know you have deep roots and will continue to grow. There has never been a day, as long as you've lived, even a bad one, that lasted longer than twenty-four hours. You will stand tall in the sun on another day. There are 365 mornings every year to start fresh and enjoy the magic of your existence.

☀ ☀ ☀

We are literally surrounded by so much beauty at all times. The sun, the sky, clouds, the sea, the stars, trees…life! We take most of it for granted on a daily basis. You are on a path that can feel overwhelming at times. But just as oxygen and sunlight sustain your very being, trials and tribulations build strength and character that will serve your greater purpose if you let them. If you believe everything happens for you and not to you, then those trials and tribulations become an aspect of the beauty that surrounds you. When you look for the opportunity for growth in every moment of your journey you will learn more about life than you ever thought imaginable and a simple walk on the beach or anywhere else in life for that matter will never be the same again.

Every moment in life is an opportunity to direct your thoughts towards the life of your dreams. When you have downtime, consider it an amazing opportunity to focus on gratitude for your skills and gifts. Express gratitude for your past, present, and future. Allow time to think about exactly what you'd like your life to look like one year from today. Read books that serve your purpose. Avoid television.

✦ ✦ ✦

While I absolutely believe the more time that we spend in life taking action on our goals and intentions, the faster they will manifest, I also believe rest and connection with nature are necessary and essential. Taking time away provides the perfect opportunity to reflect on your intentions and project the future you desire.

✦ ✦ ✦

The alchemy of a sunset is a perfect example of the magic of life. There it is, this beyond-enormous vision of beauty made up of clouds and light and wind and trees and sky. Just there existing and fading slowly into a different stage of beauty for someone else, somewhere else. It's all for you, just because you exist. Think about that for a moment.

Look up in awe. There is a satellite made of moon that has orbited the Earth for millions of years, altering tides in cycles and along with the sun and so many other factors have been creating and sustaining life so YOU could be HERE, NOW. In this lifetime. Having this conscious experience. Seems like quite a gift to waste by binge watching weekly TV shows and/or settling for anything less than the daily pursuit of a life to be passionate about.

✦ ✦ ✦

There are some days that seem to last forever and others that can't end quick enough. Some days feel so good you wish they would never end at all. But, in truth, each and every day has the exact same number of minutes. Once again, it's how we choose to spend those minutes in thought, conversation, and action that determine our perspective. When you feel as though today is a "bad day," think about all the amazing things occurring to even make that bad day possible for you to experience at all. When you choose to appreciate life for what it truly is (a perplexing and complicated constant transference of energy), you are forced to be present, and in this author's opinion, it's in our ability to be present that we are most connected to the consciousness of God.

Love, generosity, and family. There can be so much visual and emotional beauty in everything if you allow yourself to be present and take it all in. Choose your thoughts, there is a gift in every moment of life.

※ ※ ※

Life is always more beautiful on the other side of the fence. We often hear "The Grass is Greener Over There" and I think more often people believe (consciously or not) that all of life is better on the other side of something. Unfortunately, by believing that, we literally make it true.

※ ※ ※

What is Life? The answer is whatever you believe it to be. I choose to believe it is a beautiful symphony of energy to witness and mold, to observe and create. Stop waiting for life to come to you. Stop waiting for the fence to rot and fall down, so you can experience what's on the other side. The fence IS the experience. So is what is on both sides. It's all a miracle. It's all for you.

As we move through life each and every day, our actions create a sort of pre-shadow that is our future. You are in charge of what that shadow looks like. Every action you take causes a reaction in life. Remind yourself with each morning sun you see to live on purpose. Remind yourself to create the shadow you want to witness. Make your life something fun to be a part of. Stand tall. Teach others.

✦ ✦ ✦

Life is surrounding you at all times, sustaining your very existence, Gravity, sunlight, oxygen, water, sound. It is a constant and all-encompassing miracle you get to participate in. What are you doing with it? Are you serving the gift? Every single moment is literally the opportunity of a lifetime! Don't waste it.

✦ ✦ ✦

Life is a reflection of our thoughts and actions. The thoughts/actions and the reflection will serve whatever purpose we desire if we decide to be steadfast, patient, generous, and grateful in our pursuit of that purpose. To live the life of your desires, you need to take responsibility for your thoughts and actions. If you're consistent, patient, and intentional, the Universe will provide the rest!

Turn the news off. Go for a drive. Create your own scavenger hunt with things to find such as: gratitude, the sunset, opportunity for growth, beauty, laughter, life, a smile, your favorite song, stars, the moon. Live Life in the now as often as possible. The world is such a beautiful place. Life is such a beautiful thing. It's all for you.

✦ ✦ ✦

Life is so big. Why do we play so small so often? Why do we let imaginary fears of worst-case scenarios dictate the trajectory of our lives? What are you doing today to step outside your comfort zone and move more in the direction of the life of your true potential? Life is an adventure! Try something today that scares you just a little bit.

✦ ✦ ✦

Be a leader.
Follow people you admire.
Keep going.
Have fun.
Appreciate nature.

✦ ✦ ✦

Keep going. Run. Smile. Look out for one another. Breathe. Laugh.

Ryan Stanley

Where will you be in a hundred years? What are you doing in the meantime? Live Life! Create dreams and follow them. Seek joy. Seek friendship and kindness. Seek love. Create joy. Create friendship and kindness. Create love. This is not a drill.

✦ ✦ ✦

Everyone is on his or her own journey to the top. It can be a beautiful adventure with wonderful things to see. It can be cold and windy at times. Keep going. If you do it right, you'll see the world in a different way. Then you can enjoy a whole new journey of fun and adventure on the way back down.

✦ ✦ ✦

Whites become blues and blues become whites. Life is a perceptual illusion and is often only about interpretation of what lies before you. How would your life be different if you interpreted every single circumstance as one happening in your favor?

✦ ✦ ✦

Look up! Life is happening now. Seek and welcome the beauty of nature. It's everywhere.

There is beauty in nature and in history. When you stop to be present and observe, appreciating both, you can bring patience and joy into your life.

✦ ✦ ✦

Every day is an opportunity to be playful in life. When you recognize life is an infinite game, that opportunity becomes more apparent in everything you do. Treat your bed like the dug out and get out of it each day like you are taking the field. Every day is the top of another inning. How will you play the game today?

✦ ✦ ✦

Work hard and show up on purpose. When you need a break, take one. Rest your body with intention and plan your next step in your mind, with peace and awareness. You can rest and keep going at the same time. Be present while resting and embrace the rest and relaxation. Show gratitude for all of the greatness you are manifesting and the abundance of life that sustains your ability to both rest and take action. When you're ready, break your rest and step into that flow of life until it's time to rest again. There is only now.

Spend time at the end of each day thinking about something from the day you are particularly grateful for.

❖ ❖ ❖

If you always seek the beauty in the storm, you'll begin to live on purpose and recognize everything is about perspective.

❖ ❖ ❖

Take a moment to think about how much time you spend watching thirty-minute snapshots of other people's lives in "reality" or as characters compared to the amount of time you spend thirty-minute clips intentionally creating your own story for others to view in awe and wonder.

❖ ❖ ❖

Each and every day can be filled with wonder if you let it. Start with the question "What will the adventure be like today?" Then create the intention to live your day on purpose and make it wonder-full.

❖ ❖ ❖

Look up! Look down! The beauty of life is everywhere right now and it's happening for you!

Like a child growing up in your home, your subconscious is always listening to, absorbing, learning from, and acting on your words, thoughts, and actions.

※ ※ ※

There are days when it feels as though someone stole the color from your life. Those are the days when it's important to remember grey is still a color. Instead of spending your focus, time, and energy on what's missing, consider focusing your attention on gratitude for sight and for what you miss, seeking beauty and presence in the now, curious and intent on what's to come.

※ ※ ※

Life is everywhere and has been for a very long time. Occasionally, it's okay to recognize our entire existence is just a speck of dust on the side of a very, very long road. Don't take yourself so seriously.

※ ※ ※

You are certainly unique. You make a difference. Every moment is an opportunity to have an impact on the lives of several generations. But in a million years, the Earth will still be here doing its thing and we will be an archeological dig.

Ryan Stanley

Be here today and in the moment. That's all that really matters. If you spend too much time worrying about anything or everything, you're doing a disservice to the gift of now. After all, it's just life.

✦ ✦ ✦

Life is truly all about perspective. When we only look at a scenario from one perspective, we often miss out on seeing important information that could help us not only make the best decision about what is truly going on, but also what the best next steps are on our journey.

✦ ✦ ✦

Make the time to think about other perspectives before making judgments or decisions. It will not only make you more effective and efficient in your forward momentum, but also widen your mind and awareness of all that is possible.

✦ ✦ ✦

What will you build today? What will you create? A happy home? A new company? A thought leader? A new friendship? A person who lives on purpose?

Do yourself a favor and spend at least five minutes today thinking about (and possibly even writing it down) who you intend to be over the next several months, even if that's just someone who is seeking more fun. Maybe you want to spend more time in nature. Perhaps you want to spend more time with family.

✦ ✦ ✦

Make time to appreciate your surroundings today. Today is the only day like this you will ever have. Look around at all of the abundance that surrounds you and sustains your very existence. Where will the stream of life take you today?

✦ ✦ ✦

Life is all about perspective. When it feels like your world is upside down, look for the beauty in that perspective and seek the light. It's always there inside you and waiting to be seen. The more you seek it, the brighter it will shine!

✦ ✦ ✦

Beautiful? Creepy? Strong? Scary? Alone? Part of a Larger Whole? Helpful? Hindering? Awesome? Interesting? Dangerous? EVERYTHING is a perspective.

How you choose to look at each life experience is ultimately up to you. Remember that as often as you can and do your best to choose the perspective that teaches you something about life and serves your purpose.

※ ※ ※

There are so many opportunities in life to jump into something new and to trust life will be there to catch you if you fall. There are just as many opportunities to be there for others with acknowledgement and support when they are ready to take their own leap of faith.

※ ※ ※

Sometimes the path right in front of you can appear dark and scary. Know there will be lights to serve and guide you along the way. Know this part of the track is only temporary, and if you stay on it long enough, the sun will rise and you'll end up exactly where you want to be…but you have to stay on track. You have to keep going!

※ ※ ※

Nothing matters…and everything matters.

Nothing matters, meaning we're only here on this planet for a speck of time and the Universe is so big most of us really can't even comprehend when and where we actually are. So don't take everything so personally. You are not the center of the Universe. Take time to observe with wonder and amazement the beauty in the existence of your life and know a million years from now, this planet in its current way of being won't even exist.

✦ ✦ ✦

Everything matters, meaning we're only here on this planet for a speck of time. What are you doing with that one speck of time that you have? Don't take it personally with pressure and stress. It's not something to survive, because no one gets out alive. Be here now. It matters who you are now and in each moment, because that's the only moment you are experiencing.

✦ ✦ ✦

Every single day of your life is an opportunity to be present and grateful for everything and anything.

Ryan Stanley

Be who you want to be now, because that's what matters now. Don't worry about who you were, because it doesn't matter and it's not who you are now.

✦ ✦ ✦

There are lessons of strength and growth when you leap. There are lessons of understanding, compassion, and empowerment when you are there to catch someone else.

✦ ✦ ✦

Everything starts with imagination. Do you imagine yourself as a super hero in life or an average everyday person? The challenge for many of us isn't imagining who we want to be, but following through on that vision with daily intention, action, and faith it can be our reality and purpose.

✦ ✦ ✦

There are days when the weather of life gives most people a reason not to show up. If we choose to show up on purpose anyway, those are the days when we learn the most about who we are and how dedicated we are to living on purpose.

Service is so important in life. The more we serve others, the more we open ourselves up to being served. When we intentionally give and bless others with our time, energy, love, health, and money, we automatically bring joy, presence, and awareness into our own lives while simultaneously opening ourselves up to receiving more of all those things we have given.

✦ ✦ ✦

How often do you make time to be present? We work, we play, we parent, we travel, we friend, we family. Life can give you plenty to do what feels like all of the time. But it's important to stop at least three times per day to just be. To look around and create gratitude for all the things that have manifested in your life due to that working, playing, parenting, traveling, and so on. Be here now. Give thanks. Then go out and manifest more of what you want.

✦ ✦ ✦

Today is your day to bloom! Today is your day to shine! Your only purpose is to decide who you want to be in every moment. Decide who you want to be in every conversation. Decide who you want to be in every challenge. How will you bloom? How will you shine? Who will you inspire today?

FURTHER READING

Reading can be a wonderfully proactive and preventative form of first aid when you choose books/audiobooks that serve your purpose and feed your mind.

Here is a short list of some of the books I read in the past five years that have assisted me on my journey:

The Way of the Peaceful Warrior by Dan Millman

The War of Art by Steven Pressfield

Think and Grow Rich by Napoleon Hill

The Alchemist by Paulo Coelho

It Works by RHJ

The Power of Now by Eckart Tolle

Breaking the Habit of Being Yourself by Dr. Joe Dispenza

Being Peace by Thich Nhat Hanh

Notes

Notes

Ryan Stanley

About the Author

Ryan Stanley is a creative entrepreneur known for his natural ability to connect with, understand and empower people around him wherever he goes.

Since graduating from The Institute for Professional Excellence in Coaching (iPEC) in 2009 as a Certified Professional Coach (CPC) Ryan has focused most of his coaching career on musicians and others in the music industry. Ryan also spent six years working within iPEC's Admissions Department, coaching those interested in a career as a professional coach. As the Internal Coach for iPEC, Ryan coached iPEC's employees on everything from daily professional growth to how they want to show up in other more personal areas of their life. Ryan is married and has two boys. He lives in Hunterdon County, NJ. He is also a podcast host, screenwriter, speaker, and Phish fan.

Acknowlegements

To you: the reader

Thank you for making the time to read this book.

Thank you for choosing to take action and be open to thoughts and ideas that may assist you in creating the life you deserve one moment at a time.

Thank you for choosing to be patient.

Thank you for choosing to be present.

Thank you for choosing to be joyful.

Thank you for all that you do and have ever done for yourself and others.

Thanks for being you.

Keep Going.

~RMS

www.ingramcontent.com/pod-product-compliance
Lightning Source LLC
Chambersburg PA
CBHW061211070526
44583CB00025B/3209